CRAFT A WATER BOTTLE YOUR WAY!

Creating Cool Carriers for Liquids

RACHAEL L. THOMAS

CONSULTING EDITOR, DIANE CRAIG,
M.A./READING SPECIALIST

Super Sandcastle

An Imprint of Abdo Publishing
abdobooks.com

abdobooks.com

Published by Abdo Publishing, a division of ABDO, PO Box 398166, Minneapolis, Minnesota 55439. Copyright © 2020 by Abdo Consulting Group, Inc. International copyrights reserved in all countries. No part of this book may be reproduced in any form without written permission from the publisher. Super SandCastle™ is a trademark and logo of Abdo Publishing.

Printed in the United States of America, North Mankato, Minnesota
052019
092019

THIS BOOK CONTAINS
RECYCLED MATERIALS

Design: Tamara JM Peterson, Mighty Media, Inc.
Production: Mighty Media, Inc.
Editor: Megan Borgert-Spaniol
Cover Photographs: Mighty Media, Inc.; Shutterstock Images
Interior Photographs: iStockphoto; Ivo Näpflin/Flickr; Mighty Media, Inc.; que Bottle;
Shutterstock Images; US National Park Service/Wikimedia Commons

The following manufacturers/names appearing in this book are trademarks:
Bell®, Camelbak®, Elmer's® Glue-All®, Florida's Natural®, que Bottle®, Velcro®

Library of Congress Control Number: 2018967158

Publisher's Cataloging-in-Publication Data
Names: Thomas, Rachael L., author.
Title: Craft a water bottle your way!: creating cool carriers for liquids / by Rachael L. Thomas
Other title: Creating cool carriers for liquids
Description: Minneapolis, Minnesota : Abdo Publishing, 2020 | Series: Super simple diy survival
Identifiers: ISBN 9781532119729 (lib. bdg.) | ISBN 9781532174483 (ebook)
Subjects: LCSH: Outdoor recreation--Safety measures--Juvenile literature. | Survival skills--
    Juvenile literature. | Camping--Equipment and supplies--Juvenile literature. | Do-it-yourself
    work--Juvenile literature.
Classification: DDC 613.69--dc23

Super SandCastle™ books are created by a team of professional educators, reading specialists, and content developers around five essential components—phonemic awareness, phonics, vocabulary, text comprehension, and fluency—to assist young readers as they develop reading skills and strategies and increase their general knowledge. All books are written, reviewed, and leveled for guided reading and early reading intervention programs for use in shared, guided, and independent reading and writing activities to support a balanced approach to literacy instruction.

TO ADULT HELPERS

The projects in this book are fun and simple. There are just a few things to remember to keep kids safe. Some projects may use sharp or hot objects. Also, kids may be using messy supplies. Make sure they protect their clothes and work surfaces. Be ready to offer guidance during brainstorming and assist when necessary.

CONTENTS

BECOME A MAKER

A makerspace is like a laboratory. It's a place where ideas are formed and problems are solved. Kids like you create wonderful things in makerspaces. Many makerspaces are in schools and libraries. But they can also be in kitchens, bedrooms, and backyards. Anywhere can be a makerspace when you use imagination, inspiration, **collaboration**, and problem-solving!

IMAGINATION

This takes you to new places and lets you experience new things. Anything is possible with imagination!

INSPIRATION

This is the spark that gives you an idea. Inspiration can come from almost anywhere!

Makerspace Toolbox

COLLABORATION

Makers work together. They ask questions and get ideas from everyone around them. **Collaboration** solves problems that seem impossible.

PROBLEM-SOLVING

Things often don't go as planned when you're creating. But that's part of the fun! Find creative **solutions** to any problem that comes up. These will make your project even better.

SKILLS TO SURVIVE

Being a maker means being ready for anything. Your makerspace toolbox can even help you survive! People with survival skills learn to think fast and problem-solve. They find ways to stay safe and get help in **dangerous** situations.

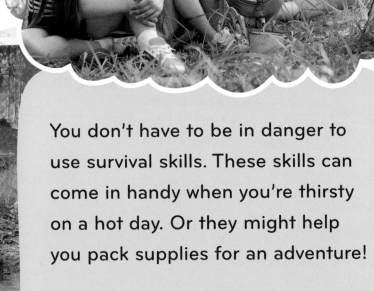

You don't have to be in danger to use survival skills. These skills can come in handy when you're thirsty on a hot day. Or they might help you pack supplies for an adventure!

PROBLEM-SOLVE!
See page 26

BASIC NEEDS

Imagine you are lost in the woods or caught in a storm. What do you do? To survive, humans must make sure their basic needs are met. When you're building gear to help you survive, keep these basic needs in mind!

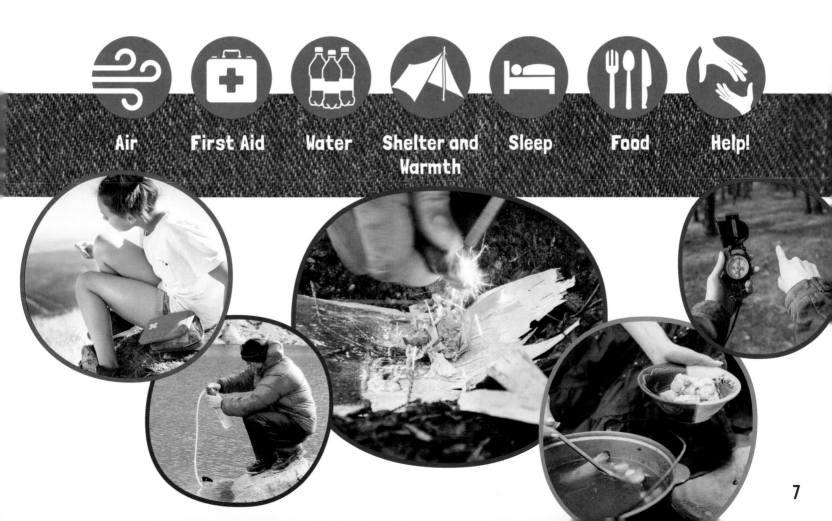

Air   First Aid   Water   Shelter and Warmth   Sleep   Food   Help!

IMAGINE A WATER BOTTLE

DISCOVER AND EXPLORE

Think of everything you drink in a day. Maybe you drink milk from a carton at lunch. Or you might gulp water from an **insulated** bottle during soccer practice. But liquid carriers can also help you stay **hydrated** while camping in the desert or climbing a mountain. And with a little creativity, they can do much more!

GET INSPIRED!
See page 24

IMAGINE

If you could **design** a cool carrier for liquid, what would it do? Would it keep water cold or warm? Could you carry it on your back for hands-free drinking? Then, imagine a situation where you need to stay **hydrated**. Are you floating in the ocean? Climbing trees in a hot jungle? Remember, there are no rules. Let your imagination run wild!

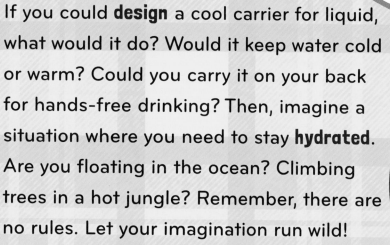

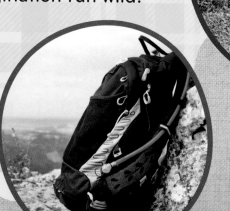

DESIGN A WATER BOTTLE

It's time to turn your dream water bottle into a makerspace marvel! Think about your imaginary liquid carrier and survival situation. How can the features of your water bottle help you survive? How could you use the materials around you to create these features? Where would you begin?

INSPIRATION

In 2016, the company que Bottle **designed** a new kind of water bottle for travel and adventure. The bottle is lightweight and **collapsible**. It can be twisted to become larger or smaller, depending on your travel needs!

COLLABORATE!
See page 28

**BE SAFE,
BE RESPECTFUL**
MAKERSPACE
ETIQUETTE

THERE ARE JUST A FEW RULES TO FOLLOW WHEN YOU ARE BUILDING YOUR WATER BOTTLE:

1. **ASK FOR PERMISSION AND ASK FOR HELP.** Make sure an adult says it's OK to make your water bottle. Get help when using sharp tools, such as a craft knife, or hot tools, like a glue gun.

2. **BE NICE.** Share supplies and space with other makers.

3. **THINK IT THROUGH.** Don't give up when things don't work out exactly right. Instead, think about the problem you are having. What are some ways to solve it?

4. **CLEAN UP.** Put materials away when you are finished working. Find a safe space to store unfinished projects until next time.

WHAT WILL YOUR WATER BOTTLE DO?

How will your water bottle help you meet your basic needs? Knowing this will help you figure out which materials to use.

Will it let you drink water hands-free? Then build a liquid carrier for your back and fit it with a stretchy straw!

Long-distance runners often wear hydration packs.

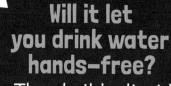

PROBLEM-SOLVE!
See page 26

IMAGINE

WHAT IF YOUR ONLY WATER SOURCE IS DEWDROPS ON PLANTS? HOW WOULD YOU COLLECT AND CARRY THIS LIQUID?

Will it let you move quickly and freely? Then divide up the water's weight over several small **containers**.

13

Sarah Marquis is an adventurer from Switzerland. From 2010 to 2013, she journeyed alone from Siberia to Australia. She walked about 10,000 miles (16,093 km)! In the Gobi Desert, Marquis gathered water to drink by collecting drops of **condensation** in a plastic bag!

Will it keep your liquids hot or cold? Then use **insulating** materials to control the liquid's temperature.

Insulating materials include wool, cotton balls, foam, and aluminum foil.

COLLABORATE!
See page 28

Will it collect and carry water over rivers or seas? Then use materials that can float and add a bowl for collecting rainwater!

⚠ STUCK?

YOU CAN ALWAYS CHANGE YOUR MIND IN A MAKERSPACE. DOES YOUR WATER RAFT KEEP SINKING? TRY ADDING WHEELS SO YOUR WATER CAN ROLL INSTEAD OF FLOAT.

BUILD YOUR WATER BOTTLE

Liquid carriers must be **watertight**. They should be **durable** and easy to carry. They should also be clean and safe to drink from. Look around for materials that could provide these features for your water bottle.

SEARCH YOUR SPACE

The perfect shape might be in your kitchen cabinet, garage, or toy chest. Search for materials that might seem surprising!

GET INSPIRED!
See page 24

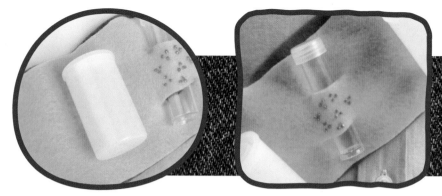

**SMALL &
SIPPABLE**

FILM CANISTER

TEST TUBE

**LARGE &
GLUGGABLE**

MILK JUG

JAR

**STRONG &
WEARABLE**

LEATHER

FELT

CONNECT YOUR WATER BOTTLE

Will your water bottle be **permanent**? Or will you take it apart when you are finished? Knowing this will help you decide what materials to use.

TOTALLY TEMPORARY

RUBBER BAND

TOOTHPICKS

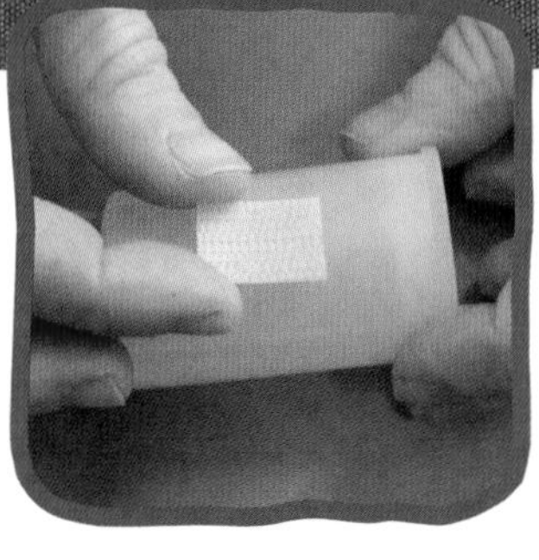

HOOK-AND-LOOP TAPE

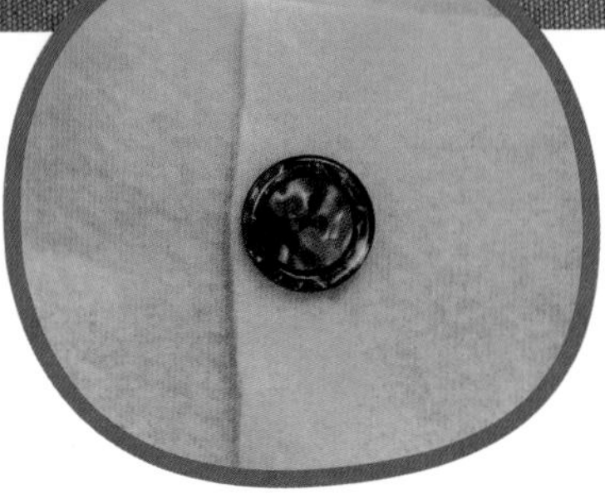

BUTTON

COLLABORATE!
See page 28

IMAGINE

WHAT IF YOU WERE IN A LAND WHERE WATER WAS AS VALUABLE AS GOLD? HOW WOULD YOU MAKE A WATER CARRIER THAT COULD BE EASILY HIDDEN FROM WATER BANDITS?

A LITTLE STICKY

CRAFT GLUE

LEATHER CORD

SUPER STICKY

HOT GLUE

NEEDLE AND THREAD

19

DECORATE YOUR WATER BOTTLE

Decorating is the final step in making your water bottle. It's where you add **details** to your liquid carrier. How do these decorations help your water bottle do its job?

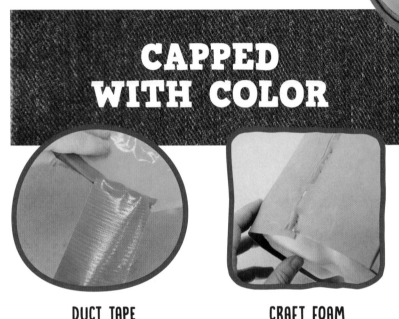

CAPPED WITH COLOR

DUCT TAPE

CRAFT FOAM

IMAGINE

WHAT IF YOU HAD TO CARRY YOUR WATER BOTTLE ON YOUR HEAD? HOW WOULD THAT CHANGE THE LOOK OF YOUR CARRIER?

GET INSPIRED!
See page 24

FUN & FUNCTIONAL

FINE DETAILS

BUTTON

CHENILLE STEM

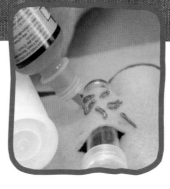

FABRIC PAINT

POM-POMS

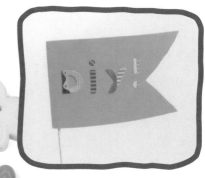

STICKERS

HELPFUL HACKS

As you work, you might discover ways to make challenging tasks easier. Try these simple tricks and **techniques** as you build your water bottle!

To make objects that can float, use materials with air pockets, such as foam noodles and bubble wrap.

Use craft glue to create an **invisible** connection. The glue is white when wet but dries clear.

Use a bowl to help shape **flexible** materials such as foil.

Make use of natural connection points, such as screw caps.

PROBLEM-SOLVE!
See page 26

To make a drawstring, poke holes through folds in your pouch. Then weave a leather cord through the holes.

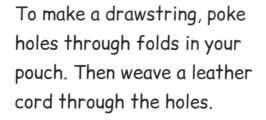

⚠ STUCK?

MAKERS AROUND THE WORLD SHARE THEIR PROJECTS ON THE INTERNET AND IN BOOKS. IF YOU HAVE A MAKERSPACE PROBLEM, THERE'S A GOOD CHANCE SOMEONE ELSE HAS ALREADY FOUND A SOLUTION. SEARCH THE INTERNET OR LIBRARY FOR HELPFUL ADVICE AS YOU MAKE YOUR PROJECTS!

Make two cuts into a folded material to create a built-in strap.

GET INSPIRED

Get inspiration from the real world before you start creating your liquid carrier!

LOOK AT THE SUPERMARKET

Supermarkets store hundreds of different liquids on their shelves. Each **container** is **designed** for a specific function. Look at these everyday containers for inspiration.

LOOK AT NATURE

Cactus plants store water in their stems. Desert spadefoot toads create a slippery body covering that traps in moisture for months. And pocket mice get most of their water from food they eat, such as seeds!

LOOK AT OUTDOOR GEAR

There are tons of water bottles **designed** for outdoor travel. Some are made from hard, lightweight materials, such as aluminum. Others are made from soft materials so they can be folded up or worn. Explore these designs to get ideas for your own liquid carrier!

25

PROBLEM-SOLVE

No makerspace project goes exactly as planned. But with a little creativity, you can find a **solution** to any problem.

FIGURE OUT THE PROBLEM

Maybe you're having trouble connecting a handle to your **insulated** carrier. Why do you think this is happening? Thinking about what may be causing the problem can lead you to a solution!

SOLUTION:
USE A STRONGER TOOL
TO BREAK THROUGH
THE PLASTIC.

SOLUTION:
USE A THICK RUBBER
BAND TO HOLD THE
HANDLE FIRMLY IN PLACE.

BRAINSTORM AND TEST

Try coming up with three possible **solutions** to any problem.

Maybe your bottle won't stand upright on your raft.

You could:

1. Use a stronger connecting material to secure the bottle to the raft.

2. Add structural elements that help support the weight of the bottle.

3. Replace the bottle with a shorter and more stable **container**, such as a jar or tin.

ADAPT

Still stuck? Try a different material or change the **technique** slightly.

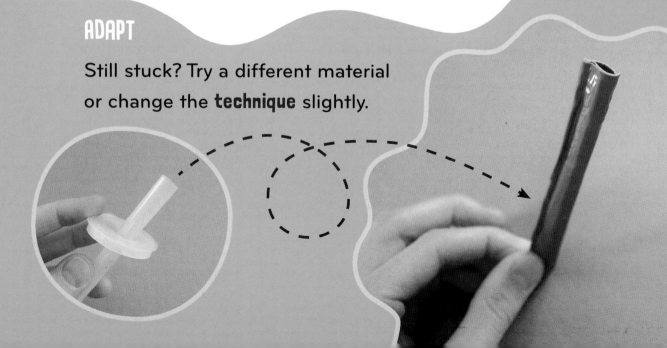

COLLABORATE

Collaboration means working together with others. There are tons of ways to collaborate to create a water bottle!

ASK A FELLOW MAKER

Don't be shy about asking a friend or classmate for help on your project. Other makers can help you think through the different steps to creating your liquid carrier. These helpers can also lend a hand during construction!

ASK AN ADULT HELPER

This could be a parent, teacher, grandparent, or any trusted adult. Tell this person about your water bottle's most important function or feature. Your grown-up helper might think of materials or **techniques** you never would have thought of!

ASK AN EXPERT

Ask players of different sports how they stay **hydrated** when they practice and compete. A salesperson at an outdoor gear store can show you what popular water bottles are made of.

THE WORLD IS A MAKERSPACE!

Your water bottle may look finished, but don't close your makerspace toolbox yet. Think about what would make your water bottle better. What would you do differently if you made it again? What would happen if you used different **techniques** or materials?

DON'T STOP AT WATER BOTTLES

You can use your makerspace toolbox beyond the makerspace! You might use it to accomplish everyday tasks, such as learning to play an instrument or running for student government. But makers use the same toolbox to do big things. One day, these tools could help create new medicines or forecast the weather. Turn your world into a makerspace! What problems could you solve?

GLOSSARY

collaborate – to work with others.

collapsible – able to fold into a smaller shape.

condensation – the liquid formed when water turns from a gas or vapor into a liquid.

container – something that other things can be put into.

dangerous – able or likely to cause harm or injury.

design – to plan how something will appear or work. A design is a sketch or outline of something that will be made.

detail – a small part of something.

durable – long lasting and able to withstand wear.

flexible – easy to move or bend.

hydrated – having enough water or moisture.

insulate – to keep heat or cold in or out. Insulation is a material that keeps heat or cold in or out.

invisible – unable to be seen.

permanent – meant to last for a very long time.

solution – an answer to, or a way to solve, a problem.

technique – a method or style in which something is done.

watertight – made so tightly that water cannot get in or out.